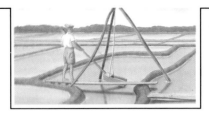

Written by Dominique Joly
Illustrated by Sylvaine Pérols

Specialist Advisers:
Salt Information Center
Salins du Midi
France

ISBN 0-944589-20-0
First U.S. Publication 1988 by
Young Discovery Library
217 Main St. • Ossining, NY 10562

YOUNG DISCOVERY LIBRARY

Grains of Salt

YOUNG DISCOVERY LIBRARY

You know what salt tastes like.
There's salt in the bread you eat. Your
food is cooked with salt. You can add it
to french fries.

**Salt is everywhere, but you can't
always see it.**

There is a lot of salt in the sea, and
under the ground. There is even salt in
the air, in a fine yellow dust. And there
is salt in soil, and in the plants that grow
in the soil.

Like sugar, salt is made up of tiny crystals. They may be transparent, or white, reddish-brown, blue or even green.

How can you recognize salt?
If you put some on the tip of your tongue, you can taste its special tangy flavor. You can crush it easily, and if you stir some into water, it disappears: it dissolves.

Our inheritance from the sea

Why do our bodies need salt?
Maybe because all life on earth began in the sea, and the salt in our bodies is an inheritance from this saltwater origin. Taste your tears next time you cry: they are salty. It is salt which regulates the amount of water there is in our bodies. But we don't need a lot of it: sometimes we eat more than we need, and this can be bad for us.

Sweat is salty. After you have been very active, you may need to eat some salt to replace what you have lost by sweating.

Where does the salt we eat come from? Salt is naturally present in most of our foods. But the extra salt we sprinkle on our food will have been extracted from the sea, or from mines under the ground.

Have you noticed that if you go swimming in the sea and then dry in the sun you are sometimes covered with a fine white crust? That is salt!

Why is the sea salty?

There are tiny traces of salt in rocks. Over millions of years, rain washes the salt out, taking it down to the sea. Water from the sea slowly evaporates, leaving salt dried up on the shore. Fresh water is added to the sea from rivers and rain. But the amount of salt in the sea as a whole hardly varies, as more salt is always being washed in.

Ever since prehistoric days, men have collected salt from the sea.

In very early times they boiled pots of seawater over a fire until only a crust of salt was left. It was the Romans who first built **salt pans.**

A salt pan consists of a number of small pools through which seawater circulates very slowly.

The pools are separated by a series of narrow dikes, linked together by small wooden trap doors.

Even today, sea salt is collected in salt pans.

Very slowly, the seawater circulates through smaller and smaller, shallower and shallower pools. It travels a long way as it passes around and around from pool to pool. By the end of its journey, the heat from the sun has made almost all the water evaporate, and the salt is left behind.

If a storm threatens, the salt collector puts the salt which is nearly ready into an enclosure so that the rainwater doesn't dilute it.

From dawn, in summer, the salt maker runs up and down the dikes, letting the water in and out. He keeps an eye on the wind, and on how hot the sun is.

When the time has come to harvest the salt, he pushes all the salt crystals which have formed towards the dike. The large, grey crystals fall to the bottom. On top, the tiny white crystals gleam in the sun.

Salt is sometimes hidden deep in the rock layers of the earth. Millions of years ago, sea covered that region. When the sea evaporated, the salt was left.

The first miners went down into the mines on ropes and carried blocks of salt up on their backs. Later on, horses carried the salt in barrels.

Later the land sank down and was covered by other rocks and soil.
The first salt mines were dug about three thousand years ago.
For people living a long way from the sea, salt mines were a great discovery.
It was very hard, working in a salt mine. Men used picks to dig out huge blocks of salt.

The heads of these picks are made of bronze.

Oil lamps hanging from the walls lit up the mines.

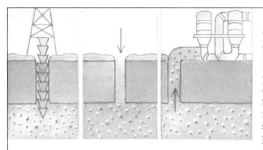

Another way of getting salt from underground: a hole is dug, water is poured in to dissolve the salt in the surrounding rocks, then the salty water is pumped out.

In past times people usually took their salt from the sea. Nowadays, most of the salt we eat is rock salt dissolved and pumped out in salty water, called **brine,** or dug out from mines.

The United States of America and China are the two biggest producers of salt in the world.

In modern salt pans, a computer works out the right time to harvest the salt. This huge pile of salt is the result of a whole year's work. The amount produced depends on the weather; a hot, dry summer means more salt.

Nowadays, the salt, obtained from salt pans, or by the pumping methods, or dug out of the mines is extracted on a massive scale, using trucks, bulldozers and explosives. One explosion in a mine can bring down five hundred tons of salt at a time. After the salt has been blasted, the pieces are put into wagons which roll along to the machines. There they are broken up and crushed, washed, sieved, and put into bags.

The salt of the desert. In some African deserts, seasonal salt lakes come and go, year after year. Where the lakes evaporate, they leave a crust of salt over the land. This salt is very precious to people living in the desert, to replace the body salt they lose by sweating.

The salty crust on the earth is cut into blocks and then carried by camel to the nearest market. Salt was once used as barter for slaves or gold and there were even coins made of salt. (When people talk of earning a 'salary', they are using a word dating from the time when Roman soldiers were paid partly in salt.)

The blocks of salt are removed with long poles.

At Fachi, in Niger, the ground is salty. Hollows are dug out, then filled with water. The water evaporates and leaves the salt.

An open air mine at Taoudenni, in Mali. Salt is cut into 130 lb. slabs and then transported by camel.

On the banks of the Great Salt Lake in Utah, the plants are encrusted with salt. It looks like snow.

A salt mountain in Rumania: the salt from underground pushes its way upwards through the rock layers, rising ½ inch a year.

Swimming in the Dead Sea: the water is so salty that you can't sink — you bob about like a cork!

The salt desert in Ethiopia. At the foot of the volcanoes, the layer of salt is fifteen thousand feet thick.

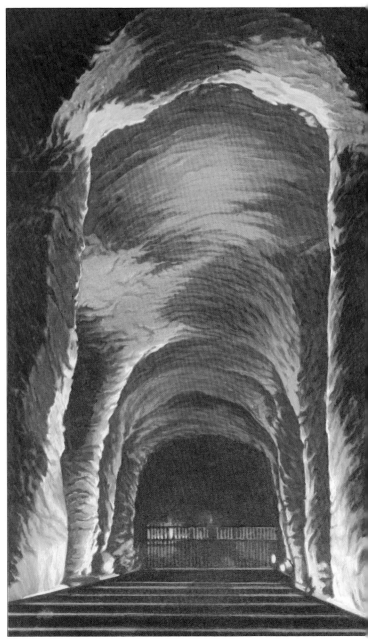

In Colombia and Poland there are churches made of salt!

The church in Colombia is at a place called Zipaquirá. It is deep underground, about thirteen hundred feet down.

To get into it you go down a winding path and then suddenly you are in a high vaulted chamber, with 20 huge pillars holding up the ceiling.

The floor, the walls, the altar and pillars are all made of salt, rubbed and polished until it gleams like translucent marble. Underneath the church, even further into the mountain, the salt is still mined.

In Wieliczka in Poland is another church where everything is made of salt — floor, stairs, even the candelabra!

This statue, made all of salt, represents the mysterious guardian of Wieliczka: the story goes that he roams the galleries — invisibly!

Salt was used to season food and make it tasty.

It was also used as a medicine.

Salt stops food from spoiling.

At the end of prehistoric times, when people started to settle in villages, they discovered that meat could be kept for several months if it was soaked in salt. Why? Salt absorbs the water in foods and dries them. It also discourages the germs that make food decay. Before refrigerators were invented, meat and fish were covered in salt to preserve them.

The Egyptians used to pluck and dress the ducks they had killed, then pack them in salt.

▶

In the Middle Ages, most of the meat the butcher sold was salted.

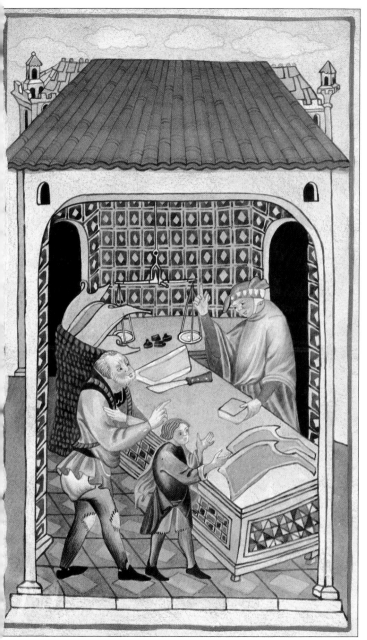

The countries of Scandinavia, in
northern Europe, did not have an
ounce of salt. Since they needed to
salt their fish and meat so that
they could eat properly the year round,
they bought it from France, Italy and
Portugal.

**Salt traveled
far and wide.**

Ships left from Venice, Italy or
southern France and sailed up to
the Baltic Sea. The salt trade was worth
a lot of money. Kings found that taxing salt
was a good way of raising money
to pay their soldiers. Almost all countries
had a salt tax, right up until the twentieth
century.

Merchants settled among themselves
how much they would charge for their salt.

Salt tax was very unpopular —
to avoid paying, people would smuggle
salt from the coast to towns inland.
But then, in the nineteenth century,
a lot of salt mines were
discovered and salt became
very cheap.

Salt
measure

Nowadays, almost every
country in the world, apart
from Scandinavia and Japan,
produces its own salt. Although
it is still invaluable,
it is no longer rare.

Barrels of salt and of wine being
carried on merchant ships in
the Middle Ages.

In times past, if you wanted to be friends with someone, you would share your bread and salt with them. Why?

Salt is the symbol of friendship and trust.

Salt was as precious as bread. In some religions, salt was sacred. Priests of Ancient Greece and Rome put salt on the sacrificial altar. Vikings put salt on the tip of a sword to welcome a new son — if the baby licked the sword, it meant he would be a great warrior.

Country people used to say that a rooster crowing meant demons were about. To send them away, a handful of salt had to be flung onto the fire. Even today, if you spill salt, some people say you should pick up a pinch with your right hand and throw it over your left shoulder to keep the devil away.

1. Salt scattered around houses was believed to keep off sickness.
2. A handful of salt on the fire was supposed to keep off storms.
3. People thought you could purify bad water by putting salt into it.

4. Salt was put on babies' tongues when they were baptized.
5. A flock was blessed with salt water to protect it.
6. In Greece, the hostess would give a guest salt before the meal.

Salt has all sorts of uses.

Can you think of some of them? Bakers always put salt into the bread they make. It helps it rise, and makes it taste good.

Salt is used to preserve fish and bacon. And have you ever tasted unsalted ham? There is no such thing! When you boil vegetables, you should always put a pinch of salt into the water — otherwise they don't taste very good.

In winter, salt is used to melt snow and ice on the roads. But it is not good for cars, because it rusts the bodywork; salty water attacks metal, particularly iron and steel.

Salt is used in water softeners. It is put into dishwashers to make the plates gleam. In fish tanks it stops algae and keeps the glass clean.

In the chemical industry, salt is king. The vital chemicals chlorine and sodium are produced from salt. It is used in processing fabrics and leather.

Look at cows and sheep in the fields in summer. They have salt licks: blocks of salt left on the ground. They need salt just as we do, and don't get enough of it from the grass they eat.

Salt used to be considered a wonder drug.

Doctors would prescribe it in ointments, powders and syrups, to cure all sorts of ills. See which ones you can spot in the picture opposite (bee stings, chest pains, toothaches, coughs, sore eyes, even laziness!). Dressings of salted nettles were put on sprains. Nowadays, salt is still useful. Use salt water as a gargle when you have a sore throat, or to soak your feet if they are swollen.

Salt box

Salt mill

Old salt cellars

But be careful with salt. You mustn't eat too much of it. It can be bad for your heart and kidneys. In the first year of their life, babies must be given as little salt as possible.

A · B · C · D · E

Make little figures from salty paste.

It is very easy. Take a mixing bowl, put in the flour and salt, and mix in the water slowly. Knead the dough for about five minutes until it is smooth. Roll it out until it is about ½ inch thick and cut shapes with scissors or a knife.

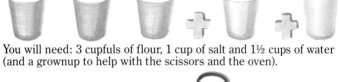

You will need: 3 cupfuls of flour, 1 cup of salt and 1½ cups of water (and a grownup to help with the scissors and the oven).

Scissors

Molds and stamps

A rolling pin

Put the shapes on a baking sheet and bake in a medium oven for 1 hour.

Take them out and let them cool, then color them with paint or felt tip pens.

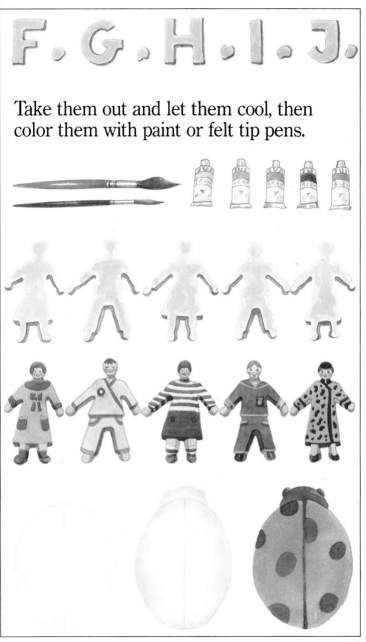

Manners of speaking:

Take it with a grain of <u>salt</u>. — I doubt it.

Worth one's <u>salt</u> — earn one's pay.

<u>Salt</u> away — to save or keep in reserve.

<u>Salt</u> down — to preserve food by adding salt.

Old <u>salt</u> — an experienced or <u>seasoned</u> sailor.

Sent to the <u>salt</u> mines — put to hard work.

He's the <u>salt</u> of the earth. — He is a fine
or noble person.

Index

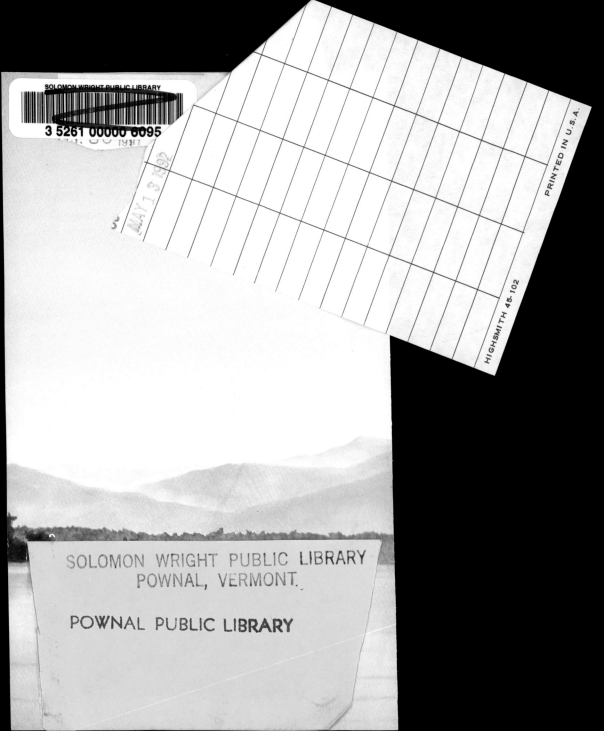